Twenty to Make

Bracelets

Amanda Walker

Search Press

First published in Great Britain 2007

Search Press Limited
Wellwood, North Farm Road,
Tunbridge Wells, Kent TN2 3DR

Reprinted 2008

Text copyright © Amanda Walker 2007

Photographs by Debbie Patterson at
Search Press Studios

Photographs and design copyright ©
Search Press Ltd. 2007

ISBN: 978-1-84448-276-4

Suppliers
If you have difficulty in obtaining any of the
materials and equipment mentioned in this book,
then please visit the Search Press website for
details of suppliers: www.searchpress.com

Dedication
For my Dad, Donald Smith.

A note on beads:

*There is a vast array of beautiful beads
available on the market and it can be
confusing working out exactly which sort
you need.*

*Beads and all related products such as
findings (all the pieces needed to connect
and assemble the jewellery; e.g. head and
eye pins and fastenings) are becoming more
readily available as the jewellery-making craft
is growing. These are generally sold in the
haberdashery department of a store or in
specialist craft shops.*

*Beads are sold in metric measurements
which give the diameter of the bead: e.g.
6mm glass pearl. Smaller beads are generally
sold by weight in grams, while larger beads
are available separately or in multiple packs.*

*Do look at the size of the threading hole
and check that the beading elastic or thread
is the right weight to fit through the holes.
Some handmade glass beads have very large
holes, but if you use a smaller bead (such as a
rocaille) on either side this will help to position
the bead correctly on the thread or elastic.
Conversely some pearls have very small
holes and the weight of thread or elastic
must be adjusted.*

*It is essential to use beading needles as the
holes in the small rocaille beads are tiny and
the eye of a general sewing needle would be
too large. Beading needles come in different
lengths depending on what kind of beading
you are doing. I generally find longer needles
to be preferable.*

Contents

Introduction   4

Sea Bride   6

Love-me-knot   8

Attraction   10

Opulence   12

Illusion   14

Eastern Princess   16

Egypt   18

Byzantine Pride   20

Cool Mint Knots   22

Poppyheads   24

Trueheart   26

Silver Zephyr   28

Rose Pearls   30

Silverfly   32

Elegance   34

Delicate Blue   36

Seaglass   38

Reflection   40

Desert Rose   42

Eye of Emerald   44

Conclusion   46

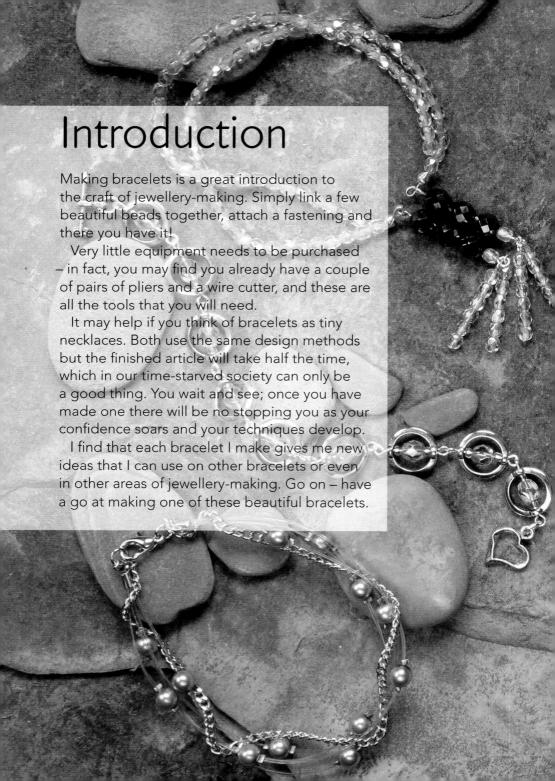

Introduction

Making bracelets is a great introduction to the craft of jewellery-making. Simply link a few beautiful beads together, attach a fastening and there you have it!

Very little equipment needs to be purchased – in fact, you may find you already have a couple of pairs of pliers and a wire cutter, and these are all the tools that you will need.

It may help if you think of bracelets as tiny necklaces. Both use the same design methods but the finished article will take half the time, which in our time-starved society can only be a good thing. You wait and see; once you have made one there will be no stopping you as your confidence soars and your techniques develop.

I find that each bracelet I make gives me new ideas that I can use on other bracelets or even in other areas of jewellery-making. Go on – have a go at making one of these beautiful bracelets.

Sea Bride

Materials:

11 x green handmade glass beads
11 x silver eye pins
1 x decorative ring and bar clasp
2 x silver jump rings

Tools:

Flat-nosed pliers
Half round-nosed pliers
Wire cutters

Instructions:

1 Thread a glass bead on to an eye pin. Using flat-nosed pliers bend the wire to a right angle and then cut, leaving 1cm of wire above the bead.

2 Using the round-nosed pliers bend the wire into a loop. Just before closing the loop fully, thread on another eye pin, then repeat this process ten more times.

3 Finally, attach a jump ring to the last eye pin, then attach the ring and bar clasp to each end of the linked beads.

Devotion

This bracelet was made using the same techniques with metal beads in place of the glass ones.

Love-me-knot

Materials:

50cm (20in) black leather lacing

1 x green luena glass bead

Tools:

Scissors

Instructions:

1 Form the lacing into a double circle. Wrap the right-hand end loosely over the doubled lacing three times, then thread the end back through the wrapped section. Pull the end tight to make a knot (see inset opposite).

2 Thread a luena bead on to the left-hand lacing end and make a second knot by wrapping the left-hand end loosely under the doubled lacing three times with the end pulled in the opposite direction approximately 10cm (4in) away from the first.

3 Trim away any excess lacing with the scissors. The knots are slip knots, making the bracelet easy to adjust to fit your wrist.

Forget-me-knot

This bracelet uses a blue luena bead for a simple alternative.

Attraction

Materials:

6 x 8mm round magnetic beads
106 x 4mm aqua faceted glass beads
4 x silver headpins
2 x eye pins
2 x calottes
50cm (20in) nylon transparent thread
    (0.25mm diameter)

Tools:

Flat-nosed pliers
Half round-nosed pliers
Wire cutters
Scissors
Beading needle
Jewellery glue

Instructions:

1 Thread the needle with the transparent thread and tie a knot approximately 10cm (4in) from the end of the beading thread.

2 Thread on forty faceted beads, then tie a knot close to the beads and cut the thread leaving a 10cm (4in) tail. Repeat the process with a second length of thread.

3 Put the two beaded threads next to each other, then pass one end of each of the threads through a single faceted bead and a calotte. Tie a few knots and dot with glue to secure the beaded thread, then close the calotte. Repeat at the other end with another faceted bead and calotte.

4 Thread two eye pins with three magnetic and one faceted bead each, then thread four headpins with six faceted beads each.

5 Using flat-nosed pliers bend the pins at right angles, then cut, leaving 1cm (¼in) of pin above the beads. Using the round-nosed pliers, bend the pin ends into loops.

6 Attach two threaded headpins to the two eye pins, then the eye pins to the calottes.

Hollywood Starlet

Simply substitute white beads for the blue beads to make this glamorous bracelet.

Opulence

Materials:

2m (79in) of light blue nylon thread
10 x 6mm tanzanite (grey) faceted glass beads
25cm (10in) of silver fine chain
4 x 4mm silver jump rings
2 x silver end caps
24 x silver crimp beads
10mm silver lobster clasp

Tools:

Flat-nosed pliers
Half round-nosed pliers
Crimping pliers
Wire cutters
Scissors
Jewellery glue

Instructions:

1 Cut eight 20cm (7¾in) lengths of nylon thread. Take two lengths and thread a crimp bead on to join them. Anchor the crimp bead in place with the crimping pliers, then thread on a faceted bead and position it with the crimp bead.

2 Slip another crimp bead on to the lengths and crimp it in place, sandwiching the bead.

3 Use crimp beads to secure two more beads along the pair of threads to complete the length.

4 Make one more nylon thread pair in the same way with three beads, and two pairs with two beads.

5 Glue the ends of the four pairs of beaded threads together, then encase them inside the end caps.

6 Loosely wrap the chain around the threads. Attach jump rings to the end caps and chain ends and then attach the lobster clasp.

Purity

Using lime green glass pearls and changing the colour of the other materials can create a very different effect. Try changing the number of beads (as shown below) for another simple variation.

Illusion

Materials:

6 x 16mm black wrapped beads
27 x 10mm steel glass pearls
70 x 4mm half silver crystal faceted glass beads
44cm (17¾in) of platinum fine chain
Silver spring fastening
4 x silver jump rings
2 x 4mm silver end caps
1m (36in) of 0.25mm nylon transparent thread
Silver extension chain with heart

Tools:

Flat-nosed pliers
Half round-nosed pliers
Wire cutters
Scissors
Beading needle
Jewellery glue

Instructions:

1 Thread the needle with the transparent thread and tie a knot approximately 10cm (4in) from the end. Thread on fifty faceted beads, tie a knot close to the beads to secure them and then cut the thread leaving a 10cm (4in) tail.

2 Take another length of thread, tie a knot 10cm (4in) from the end and thread on a faceted glass bead, then twenty glass pearls and then another faceted glass bead. Tie a knot close to the bead and cut the thread, leaving a 10cm (4in) tail.

3 Thread a third length with the remaining faceted beads, alternating glass pearls and wrapped beads between pairs of faceted beads.

4 Pass all three threads through a single faceted bead, tie in a knot, place a dot of glue on the knot and encase in an end cap. Repeat on the other end.

5 Cut the chain in half and attach in two strands to jump rings; attach the rings behind the single faceted beads.

6 Attach jump rings to the end caps, then the fastening and extension chain.

Neptune's Treasure

Using copper materials rather than silver, and ivory rather than black wrapped beads will give you a bracelet with a vintage style.

Eastern Princess

Materials:

36cm (14in) of 3.5cm (1¼in) wide ivory
   transparent ribbon

7 x silver drum eye divider beads

6 x silver ring diamond divider beads

3 x salmon (pink) luena glass beads

4 x handmade glass beads

6 x 6mm silver round fantasy metal beads

8 x 4mm silver crystal faceted glass beads

2 x 6mm silver end caps

9 x 4mm silver jump rings

Horseshoe-shaped ring and bar clasp

7 x headpins

Tools:

Flat-nosed pliers

Half round-nosed pliers

Wire cutters

Scissors

Instructions:

1 Cut the ribbon into two 18cm (7in) lengths and hold the lengths together. Starting with a drum eye divider bead, thread on seven drum eye metal divider beads, alternating them with six ring diamond divider beads.

2 Gather both ends of the ribbon and encase them in the end caps, then attach jump rings.

3 Attach the horseshoe ring and bar clasp to the jump rings.

4 Thread a headpin with a faceted bead, a handmade glass bead and another faceted bead. Repeat with three more headpins.

5 Thread a headpin with a round metal bead, a salmon luena bead and another metal bead. Repeat with two more headpins. Using flat-nosed pliers, bend the wires at right angles, then cut, leaving 1cm (¼in) of wire above the beads.

6 Using the round-nosed pliers, bend the wires into loops and attach these to the drum eye beads with jump rings.

Butterfly

Rather than use headpins, you can simply attach butterfly charms to the drum divider beads using jump rings.

Egypt

Materials:
5 x turquoise-wrapped 16mm beads

10 x 16mm bead caps

10 x 4mm aqua faceted glass beads

5 x eye pins

5cm (2in) of fine gold chain

Gold extension chain with heart and
   lobster clasp

Tools:
Flat-nosed pliers

Half round-nosed pliers

Wire cutters

Instructions:

1 Put two bead caps on one of the turquoise wrapped beads, then thread it on to an eye pin between two faceted beads (see inset opposite).

2 Using flat-nosed pliers, bend the wire to a right angle and then cut, leaving 1cm (¼in) of pin above the beads. Using the round-nosed pliers, bend the wire into a loop. Just before closing the loop fully, thread on another eye pin prepared in the same way.

3 Repeat this process five times.

4 Cut two 2.5cm (1in) lengths of chain using the wire cutters. Open the loop of the eye pin at each end and attach the chain.

5 Open the last link of each piece of chain and attach the lobster clasp and the extension chain.

Orient

For this opulent black bracelet, thread on 6mm gold metal beads instead of the faceted beads.

Byzantine Pride

Materials:

40cm (15¾in) of gold chain

1 x large gold ring
and bar clasp

3 x gold headpins

10 x 6mm gold metal fantasy
spintop round beads

1 x pink glass handmade bead

3 x 8mm gold jump rings

6 x gold rocailles

Tools:

Flat-nosed pliers

Half round-nosed pliers

Wire cutters

Instructions:

1 Use the pliers to open out the last links on the ends of the chain and attach them to the ring and bar clasp.

2 Fold the gold chain in half and attach the fold to the ring and bar clasp in the same way.

3 Thread two of the gold headpins with two rocailles and then four gold metal beads and the remaining headpin with two rocailles and a pink handmade bead sandwiched between two gold beads.

4 Using flat-nosed pliers, bend the pins at right angles, then cut, leaving 1cm (¼in) of wire above the beads. Use the round-nosed pliers to bend the wires into loops.

5 Attach jump rings to each pin and then attach the jump rings to the ring of the clasp to complete the bracelet.

Aspiration

This bracelet shows what a difference a simple change of colour can make to the finished bracelet.

Cool Mint Knots

Materials:

56cm (22in) of black leather lacing

4 x green glass handmade beads

2 x silver metal beads

1 x pendant metal bead

12 x 2mm silver-lined clear rocailles

8 x 4mm silver jump rings

1 x 8mm silver jump rings

2 x 6mm silver end caps

1 x silver spring fastening

Tools:

Flat-nosed pliers

Half round-nosed pliers

Wire cutters

Scissors

Instructions:

1 Cut the leather lacing in half and hold the two halves together. Using them as one strand, make a loop and take the free ends over and through the loop to make a knot near the middle.

2 Tie a second knot 2.5cm (1in) from the other, taking the free ends under and through the loop to make a knot that faces the other way (see inset opposite). Encase both sets of free ends in the end caps.

3 Attach two 4mm jump rings and then the spring fastening to the end caps.

4 Thread four handmade glass beads and two metal beads on to separate heads pins, threading a rocaille on each side of the beads.

5 Using flat-nosed pliers, bend the pins at right angles then cut them, leaving 1cm (¼in) of wire above the beads.

6 Use the round-nosed pliers to bend the wires into loops. Attach the 8mm jump ring to the metal pendant bead to make a pendant.

7 Divide the threaded headpins into two groups, with two glass beads and one metal bead in each group. Thread each group on to a separate jump ring.

8 Link two jump rings together, attaching the assembled jump rings to each end. Link another jump ring to one end and then attach this ring to the leather lacing between the knots, with the remaining metal bead attached to it with the final jump ring.

Fly-by-night

Made in exactly the same way as the bracelet opposite, dusky pink tanzanite beads replace the green glass beads in this variation.

Poppyheads

Materials:

- 9 x mixed pink fashion beads
- 8 x silver diamond-patterned metal divider ring beads
- 2 x silver dot-patterned metal divider drum beads
- 60cm (24in) artificial leather lacing in pink

Tools:

Scissors

Darning needle

Instructions:

1 Thread the darning needle with the 60cm (24in) length of artificial lacing, and thread a metal dot-patterned drum bead on to the lacing.

2 Thread the nine fashion beads with metal dividers between each and then the remaining dot-patterned drum bead (see inset opposite).

3 Centre the beads, evening out the lacing tails. The bracelet is fastened by tying the threaded lacing around the wrist with a bow.

Apple Blossom

Green fashion beads make a more subtle but equally striking variation on the bracelet.

Trueheart

Materials:

1 x copper metal bracelet
6 x metal copper hearts
28 x 4mm metal bronze faceted glass beads
13 x copper headpins

Tools:

Flat-nosed pliers
Half round-nosed pliers
Wire cutters

Instructions:

1 Thread six headpins with the copper hearts, then bend the pins at right angles using flat-nosed pliers. Cut the wire, leaving 1cm (¼in) above the beads.

2 Using the round-nosed pliers, bend the wires into loops.

3 Thread seven headpins with four faceted bronze beads each (see inset opposite). Bend, cut and loop the ends of the pins in the same way as the pins with hearts.

4 Thread these assembled headpins alternately on to the copper bracelet.

Opulence

This variation uses single decorative beads in place of the faceted bronze beads. In addition, the metal flowers and decorative beads are sandwiched between rocailles.

Silver Zephyr

Materials:

9 x assorted handmade blue glass iris beads

7 x silver metal dot-patterned divider drum beads

6 x silver metal diamond-patterned divider ring beads

1 x open cross charm

2 x 6mm silver metal fantasy round beads

3 x silver headpins

4 x 8mm silver jump rings

20cm (7¾in) of nylon transparent elastic

20cm (7¾in) of 0.25mm nylon transparent thread

Tools:

Flat-nosed pliers

Half round-nosed pliers

Wire cutters

Scissors

Beading needle

Jewellery glue

Instructions:

1 Thread a beading needle with a short length of thread, double over and tie the two ends in a knot. Pass the needle through one of the metal beads, leaving a loop of thread on the other side of the bead.

2 Thread the elastic into this loop and then pull the needle and thread fully through the bead which in turn pulls the elastic through as well. Thread the seven glass and the thirteen metal beads using the photograph opposite as a guide.

3 Knot the two ends of the elastic firmly together, placing a dot of glue on to the knot.

4 Thread two headpins with the remaining glass beads. Using flat-nosed pliers bend the pins at right angles, then cut, leaving 1cm (¼in) of wire above the beads.

5 Thread the last headpin with the last drum bead sandwiched between the two 6mm metal fantasy round beads. Using flat-nosed pliers bend the pins at right angles, then cut, leaving 1cm (¼in) of wire above the beads.

6 Using the round-nosed pliers bend the wires into loops. Attach a jump ring to each of the prepared headpins and one to the metal cross charm.

7 Attach the jump rings to the elastic between the metal beads (see inset opposite).

Genie

Handmade glass beads make distinctive jewellery because of their unique shapes.

Rose Pearls

Materials:

18cm (7in) heavy silver chain
1 x large silver ring and bar clasp
8 x 12mm dusky pink glass pearls
8 x silver headpins

Tools:

Flat-nosed pliers
Half round-nosed pliers
Wire cutters

Instructions:

1 Open out the last links on the ends of the chain and attach them to the ring and bar clasp.

2 Thread eight headpins with the glass pearls. Use flat-nosed pliers to bend the pins at right angles, then use the wire cutters to trim them, leaving 1cm (¼in) of wire above the beads.

3 Thread a pin end through a link on the chain and then use the round-nosed pliers to bend the wire into a loop.

4 Repeat this process with the remaining seven threaded pins, spacing the beads evenly along the chain.

Harvest

Olive green pearls give a restful, natural look to this bracelet.

Silverfly

Materials:

16cm (6¼in) medium weight silver chain

1 x silver extension chain with heart and lobster clasp

6 x cone charms

6 x dragonfly charms

6 x open cross charms

6 x butterfly charms

6 x 8mm lacing beads with eyes

31 x silver jump rings

Tools:

Flat-nosed pliers

Half round-nosed pliers

Wire cutters

Instructions:

1 Using the pliers, open out thirty jump rings and then thread each with one of the metal charms.

2 Attach each jump ring to a link of the chain (see inset opposite) by closing the jump rings with the pliers.

3 Attach a jump ring to one end of the chain and the lobster clasp to the ring and the extension chain to the other end.

Allsorts

Threading thirty headpins with glass beads in place of the metal charms gives a very different effect.

Elegance

Materials:

1 x leather strap
1 x 9mm two-piece fastening
3 x round flower leather slips
2 x 18mm hourglass leather slips
3 x craft jewels

Tools:

Hammer
Tweezers
Jewellery glue

Instructions:

1 Slide one of the flower slips into the middle of the leather strap, then slide an hourglass slip on either side.

2 Slide the remaining flower slips on to either side to make the pattern shown in the photograph opposite.

3 Use jewellery glue to attach a large craft jewel to the centre of each of the flower slips. When the glue has dried, slide on the fastening, place the rivets into the holes and use a hammer to knock the rivets home on a firm surface.

Chic Crystals

The variety of leather slips available means that it is very easy to create your own unique design. Here I have used various square and rectangular slips and decorated them with different arrangements of craft jewels.

Delicate Blue

Materials:

28cm (11in) silver chain

3 x dark blue luena glass beads

4 x 7mm silver fantasy spintop beads

2 x silver headpins

Tools:

Flat-nosed pliers

Half round-nosed pliers

Wire cutters

Instructions:

1 Thread two spintop metal beads with a luena bead in between on to each of the headpins (see inset opposite). Bend the pins at right angles using the flat-nosed pliers, then cut the pins, leaving 1cm (¼in) of wire above the beads.

2 Thread the ends of the pins through the ends of the chain and then use the round-nosed pliers to bend the pin ends into loops.

3 Double the chain up and then slide the remaining bead on to the chain by taking the folded chain through the bead.

4 Place the loop of chain around your wrist and then loosely knot the chain under the bead, pulling the chain to the desired length.

Tiger's Eye

Use warmer-toned beads for a more exotic look, like this beautiful yellow bracelet.

Seaglass

Materials:

5.5m (216½in) of 1mm aqua imitation
    leather cord
32 x assorted handmade glass iris beads

Tools:

Scissors
Darning needle
Jewellery glue

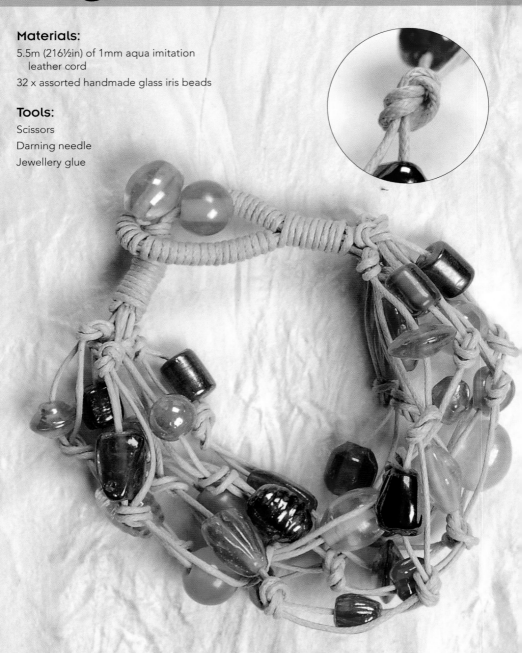

Instructions:

1 Cut six 80cm (31½in) lengths of cord. Fold one length in half and then tie a knot 5cm (2in) down from the folded end by making a loop, taking the ends through the loop and pulling the cords tight (see inset opposite).

2 Thread a glass bead on to just one of the cords of the pair, then tie a knot in both the cords 3cm (1¼in) away from the first. Repeat this with four more beads along the paired cord.

3 Repeat the whole process with the remaining five lengths of cord, alternating the colour of the beads.

4 To make the binding loop, gather the folded ends together and glue all the strands together just above the first knots. Wrap cord around the glued area for 1cm (¼in), then separate the strands into two bunches.

5 Wrap cord around the loop that this forms. When you reach the end of the loop, thread the cord on to a darning needle. Pass the needle through the centre of the bound area; pull tightly and cut the end of the cord.

6 On the other end of the piece, thread two beads on to separate cords, double the cords over and then stick all the strands together 1cm (¼in) above the knots.

7 Cut the cords to 2cm (¾in) long. Bind over the glued area to just below the beads. Thread the cord end on to a darning needle. Pass the needle through the centre of the bound area.

8 Pull tightly and cut the end of the cord.

Constellation
This alternative shows how the bracelet looks with only one type of bead rather than a mixture.

Reflection

Materials:

9 x silver rings with two eyes
9 x 6mm aqua faceted glass beads
18 x silver lined rocailles
9 x silver eye pins
2 x silver jump rings
1 x bow-and-arrow ring and bar clasp

Tools:

Flat-nosed pliers
Half round-nosed pliers
Wire cutters

Instructions:

1 Thread an eye pin through the first hole of a silver ring, then thread a rocaille, glass bead and rocaille on to the eye pin before taking the pin through the second hole of the silver ring.

2 Using flat-nosed pliers, bend the pin to a right angle and then cut the pin with wire cutters, leaving 1cm (¼in) of wire above the ring and bead.

3 Using the round-nosed pliers, bend the pin into a loop. Just before closing the loop fully, thread on another eye pin and repeat this sequence of rings and beads eight more times.

4 Attach a jump ring to each end and then the ring and bar clasp to the jump rings.

Ardent Truth
The diamond flower beads used below fit the silver rings perfectly.

Desert Rose

Materials:

20cm (7¾in) fine silver chain

27 x 4mm tanzanite (grey) faceted glass beads

3 x 6mm tanzanite (grey) faceted glass beads

3 x silver metal beads

3 x pink handmade glass beads

1 x end cap with decorative edging

9 x 2mm silver lined clear rocailles

3 x silver headpins

3 x silver jump rings

1 x small silver ring and bar clasp

2 x calottes

40cm (15¾in) of 0.25 mm nylon transparent thread

Tools:

Flat-nosed pliers

Half round-nosed pliers

Beading needle

Jewellery glue

Wire cutters

Scissors

Instructions:

1 Thread the needle with nylon thread and fold it in half; pass the cut ends through a calotte, tie a few knots, dot with glue and then close the calotte.

2 Thread the following on to the doubled thread: twenty-seven faceted beads, then a rocaille on either side of two metal, one glass and three large faceted beads, threaded alternately.

3 Pass the needle through the remaining calotte, tie a few knots, dot with glue and then close the calotte.

4 Thread three headpins with the remaining pieces. Use flat-nosed pliers to bend the pins at right angles, then cut, leaving 1cm (¼in) of wire above the beads.

5 Using the round-nosed pliers, bend the pin ends into loops. Attach these pins to a jump ring, then the ring and bar clasp to each end.

6 Cut the chain in two, attach a jump ring to each end, and attach one of these rings to the ring of the clasp and the other to the end of the small threaded faceted beads.

Sea of Tranquillity

This bracelet, like the one on the facing page, is simple to make, despite looking intricate.

Eye of Emerald

Materials:

10cm (4in) of fine silver chain
2 x silver rings with two eyes
4 x 6mm peridot (pale green) faceted beads
1 x light green handmade large glass bead
2 x 14mm silver bead caps
2 x 4mm crystal half-silver faceted glass beads
4 x silver headpins
1 x silver eye pin
1 x 7mm spring ring fastening

Tools:

Flat-nosed pliers
Half round-nosed pliers
Wire cutters

Instructions:

1 Thread an eye pin with a crystal faceted bead, a bead cap, a large glass bead, then another bead cap and faceted bead.

2 Using flat-nosed pliers bend the pin to a right angle and then cut, leaving 1cm (¼in) of wire above the ring and bead. Bend the pin into a loop using the round-nosed pliers.

3 Thread two headpins through the inside of a ring with two eyes, then thread a larger faceted bead on to each.

4 Bend and cut the headpin before threading on half of the fine chain and bending into a loop to secure it to the chain. Attach the other pin to the assembled large central bead. Repeat this process to the other side of the centre bead.

5 Attach the spring fastening by opening the end links of the chain.

Titania's Charm

While it has been made in an identical way to the Eye of Emerald, this bracelet uses restful pink beads rather than the striking green emerald beads for a markedly different effect.

Conclusion

I hope you have enjoyed the book and that it has encouraged you to have a go. As you can see, some of the bracelets will take you just minutes to make, giving you a sense of achievement that will spur you on to the next project.

Start collecting beads, and so long as you have a good collection of headpins, eye pins, fastenings and so forth, you will be ready to start when the mood takes you. I hope the designs in this book have inspired you to develop your own style and creativity when making your own bracelets.

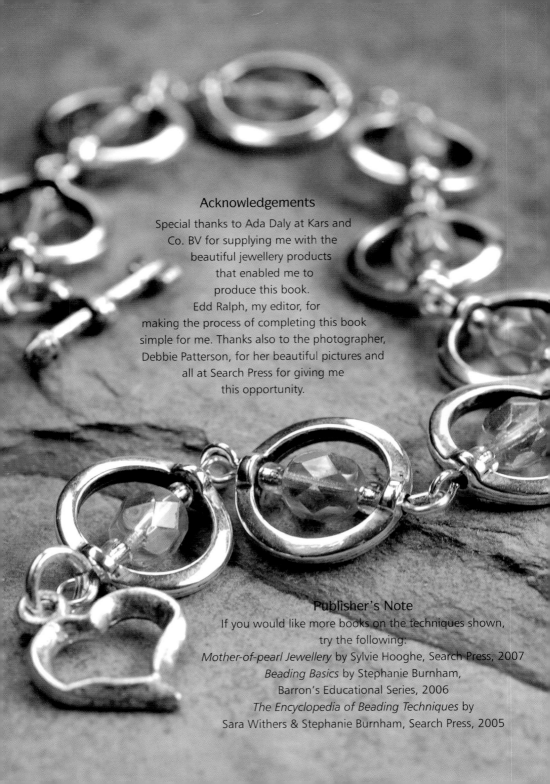

Acknowledgements

Special thanks to Ada Daly at Kars and
Co. BV for supplying me with the
beautiful jewellery products
that enabled me to
produce this book.
Edd Ralph, my editor, for
making the process of completing this book
simple for me. Thanks also to the photographer,
Debbie Patterson, for her beautiful pictures and
all at Search Press for giving me
this opportunity.

Publisher's Note
If you would like more books on the techniques shown,
try the following:
Mother-of-pearl Jewellery by Sylvie Hooghe, Search Press, 2007
Beading Basics by Stephanie Burnham,
Barron's Educational Series, 2006
The Encyclopedia of Beading Techniques by
Sara Withers & Stephanie Burnham, Search Press, 2005